Sunshine Superman

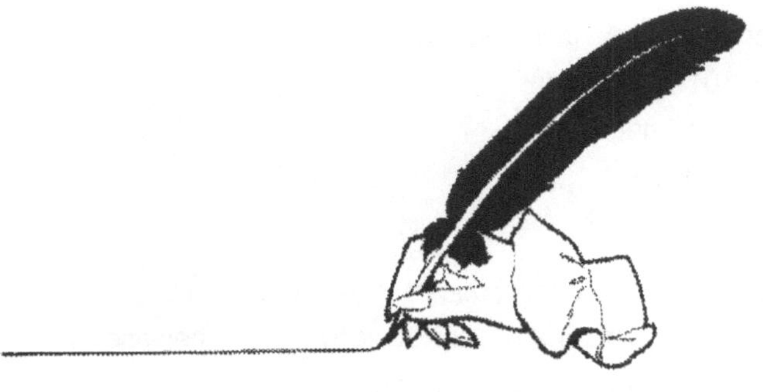

Alan Catlin

Acknowledgements

Sunshine Superman appeared in Wisconsin Review, Depression and Ode, "Some velvet morning when I'm straight…..and Like the songs we used to hear on late night radio in Art Mag, Three Stooges Celebrate Halloween and Driver's Ed in Screed, Poor Boy at School in Poesy, The Times They Are a Changin' in Clark Street, "Drugs, Sex and Rock n Roll" in Lines, Summer of Love in Hampden Sydney Poetry Review, Coming Home 1968 in Third Lung, It was just another winter appeared on line in Rusty Truck reprinted in Doubly Mad , Walking Home in Winter 1969 and "I read all the books about the lives of the boys" also accepted for Doubly Mad, Season of the Witch appeared on line in Dead Snakes, Trout Fishing in America's in James River Review, Walking Home Winter 197- at Radiant Turnstile

Contents

Sunshine Superman

for DC

was one of the handles
he gave himself, dressing up
as some kind of total hippie,
freak power dude: layers of
love beads on his open at
the neck, loose fitting smock,
shirt, hairless chest exposed
loud yellow, matching bell
bottom pants decorated
with flowers, paisleys, granny
glasses with off-color tinted
lenses, not quite concealing lost-
in-a-dark-muddle-of-bad-dream
acid, tripping through dormitories,
handing out free samples for
his drug of the month club,
spreading artificial cheer like
a demented Pied Piper of Upstate
New York with a hash pipe instead
of a flute to entice the children
to follow after where he was
going at the speed of unseen light,
picking out his final resting place
among the crypts and mausoleum
he stalked late at night, when his
drugs of the moment, and the full
moon were peaking at the same time.

Dormitory Living Late 60's; A Still Life, Utica, N.Y.

Long before "The Shining"
there was Utica, lake and
valley effects, snow piles,
drifts two stories high,
campus paths sheer ice sheen
on blacktop between snow
blown banks, white fields
polar ice capped, nearest
buildings off-campus, a mile
and a lifetime away, a locked
down-for-all-seasons asylum
for those certifiably lost, wards
of the state, foundering,
hopeless, the future homeless
of America; house lights dim
every time they apply the electro-
shock machine, twin funnels
of steam, smoke, silhouetted
against perpetually gray sky.

Insomniac

First deep frost by late
October, bare, ruined trees
in the graveyard behind
the new dormitory & just
beyond, in open fields, Crazy
John wanted to shoot Wild Turkeys,
Quail. Said he could see
himself stalking game by
a Harvest Moon's light
or at sunrise, fog blankets
lifting the white bark from
leafless trees, his thick, gray
shadow darker than all the others,
sliding behind marble stones,
crypts, weapon locked & loaded.
That was beyond stupid, everyone
agreed, even him, we thought,
though just this side of dreams,
maybe asleep, maybe awake, I swear
I could hear shots.

A West Side Story in East Utica

The blonde at the bar eyed
new arrivals, sized them up,
chose one and sidled up close,
whispered like something out
a 60's pop hit, "You look like
my kind of man." Leaned forward
and gave him a kiss with a tongue
in it, "Buy me a beer and we'll talk.
Who knows, we might have a lot
in common. Don't go anywhere,
I'll be back."

"Sure. Why not?" he thought,
"Dos cervezas, por favor."
He said to the nearest barman,
watching her as she walked away.
"You sure that's what you want to do?
No skin off my ass if you do but
you might want to think about it."
"Sure, why not?"
"Maybe you were born irresistible,
I don't know. You look kind of average
to me, but I could be wrong. You might
have a hidden weapon only the ladies
know about, which is neither here nor
there to me. Just wondering if you're
used to women falling all over you like that."
"It happens."
"Sure it does. Look, you notice two

guys in the parking lot going at it in
the parking lot outside?"
"I saw some kind of beef. Wasn't none
of my business so I just moved on."
"Well, it was your business, in a way."
"How's that? I don't know those guys."
"Hell, I doubt they know each other.
See they were having an argument over
a woman. A blonde woman. A very forward
blonde woman. A teasing bitch of a blonde.
You figure one of them is bound to turn up
in here eventually, when they're done
making pin cushions out of each other."
"I see. Maybe you're right. One beer
is good. She's not that hot anyway."

Depression: an Ode 1967

Summer nights I sat
drinking a bottle of
Ballantine eight year
old, straight from the fifth,
listening to the Moonlight
Sonata, a fugue for a poet
with no words, for a pianist,
with carpal tunnel "Electric
Prunes rock!" he'd said in
an interview before a concert
when he could still play
Beethoven, Chopin, Schumann,
a curtain call Prokofiev toccata
guaranteed to bring the listeners
to their feet. And the long lost
girl who said, "All the poet's
songs are sad ones, are the ones
with refrains like 'too much of nothing
makes a man ill at ease...' or
'melt back into the night, babe,
everything in here is made of stone'
or 'I had too much to dream last night....'"
Too much to dream. Last night,
every night, each unwritten sentence
eight years long begins, "Hello, darkness my
old friend...."as if each poem were
something that could only be composed
while paralyzed on the death bed of love.

The Roommate

"Such a weekend there
never was." he'd say,
crawling on all fours down
the dormitory hall, his white
shirt torn and soiled by who
knows what, pants ripped out
at both knees, carpet burns
beneath showing through rent
fabric. Ten minutes after his
arrival, Tennessee Shit kicking
hillbilly music would blast
from his room, though it was
fairly well known, he was
bred, born and raised in Boston
Brahmin. No doubt, he'd
acquired his chaw chewing
habits elsewhere and the music?
Who knew? More than once,
his roomie would alert the floor,
"Joe's dead! You've got to help
me pull him out of the shower
before he drowns." These two,
a strange alliance of altar boy
and gutter snipe, a pairing only
the cruel gods of the Dormitory
Authority could arrange. Despite
Joe's mistaking roomie's desk
drawer for a pot to puke in,

his closet for a stand-up urinal,
theirs was an odd combination
that worked; Mother Hen and
delinquent child, each suited to
the other by their particular needs.

Three Stooges Celebrate Halloween

They carried shot
glasses door to door
imploring, "Trick or
Drink" to astonished
homeowners who
either couldn't take
a joke or could,
filling their glasses
with what was on
hand: store brand
Vodka, no name
English Gin, Dark
Puerto Rican Rums,
Old Rot Gut Rye,
Bourbon, Scotch—'til
they were three stooges
stumbling over sidewalk
cracks, low curbs,
Elm tree roots, sick in
nearby shrubs or behind
parked cars, white as
spirit ghosts set free
for a day of the dead.

Poor boy at school

he came along
for all the wild,
crazy rides to
the end of night,
no money for
beers or booze,
partial scholar-
ships don't cover
alcohol consumption
in seedy college bars
listening to Mustang
Sally, wanting a
woman, wanting
everything he didn't
have, wanting out.
Enlisted in the Navy,
shipping out overseas
in '67 seemed better
than penniless in Utica,
always 30 below,
inside and out,
until the sniper
round that wanted
you dead like that
Uncle Sam poster
on Roomie's wall,
found a home.
The leaves were
still on the trees

when we heard
what hit you.
Doc said sophomore
year was going to
be hell & he was
right.

Driver's Ed

"It was pissing rain &
shitting snow & I must
have been doing 90 maybe
a 100 flat out, who really
knew or cared? when
the red lights start flashing
behind me, I thought about
maybe making a run for it
but I decided not to...I just
didn't feel as if my time was
used up yet so I pulled over,
got my license & stuff ready...
Well, as you might imagine,
he was sure as hell pissed
to be out there in all that rain
& shit, sd., something to
the effect of, "Didn't anyone ever
tell you about defensive driving?
Do you know how fast you were
going?" So, I sd., "Yes, officer,
actually I did know, more or less.
The way I look at it, there can't be
any defensive drivers without
offensive drivers & I'm one of those,"
Somewhere along the line, in his
academic career, the Statie must
have studied Philosophy or Ethics
or whatever this fell under...
He got this disgusted look on

his face, tossed by license & shit
through the window and sd.,
"Get the hell out of here before
I change my mind."
"Don't mind if I do." I sd. but
I didn't push it by suggesting that
he have a nice day or something
like that. I may act it, but I'm
not completely insane.

It was just another winter

of Bob Dylan and death
nineteen sixty whatever
and the kid who sat next
to me in Medieval History
had jumped off the Hotel Utica
after mid-term failing grades
had gone out and no one would
sit in that seat as if they too might
go over the edge or that the chair
was haunted by his spirit, the same
kind of spirit I saw in her eyes
dancing close to me, to "Like a
Rolling Stone", the long version,
at some beer blast just this side of
ice hell, vocals by some local loser
who couldn't carry a tune, hold a note,
but who knew all the words which is
what I was listening for, her body so
close to mine, I thought we were almost
one, both of her arms, her hands locked
around my neck, her lips on mine,
her tongue, and then she was saying,
"Love me just like a woman."
And I wondered who her fancy man was,
wondered where he had gone and why me?
The scent of her, the taste, this girl
from the north country, like the Dylan
folk song I loved, but where was I?
My head full of confusion boats,

crazy dreams and cheap beer,
incapable of love. "I can't." I said.
"Make believe," she said, "and I will too."
Then she kissed me hard and long
and deeply as if she really meant it.

The Transfer Student from Hell 1968

No one had seen him
since the start of
the semester though you
could hear him, scratching
on the walls, scuttling
amid the rubble presumed
to be inside, knocking
things unknown over,
dragging stuff across
the floor, something
screeching that could
have been a living thing
tortured or a recording
of the worst kind of
suffering known to man.
If he went to classes he
left the room under cover
of complete darkness long
after everyone should have
been sleeping. DC said
he'd seen this pale-as-death-
person dressed all in black
walking on frozen snow banks,
gesturing toward the full
moon, his arms outstretched
summoning reflected light,
alternate life sources he
intended to assume as his
own. Doc sd. DC's out of

his mind and everyone agreed,
he was, but what he had said
went a long ways toward
explaining whatever it was
that was happening behind
that closed, that double locked
door.

The Times They Are a Changing':

Summer Late 60's, Death & Transfiguration Blues

Brush cuts and slacks transformed
into long hair & bell bottoms, jeans
patched over worn through holes,
ripped fabrics becoming functional
art forms, wearable works in progress,
underage drinking pints of cheapest
Vodka available to young men, drinking
it straight or with warm Coke mixtures
replaced by roll-your-own dabs,
communal water pipes, filtration systems
containing bottom shelf white wine,
sharing a smoke of many dreams, deep
sixing beers, wild laughter in the dark,
near hysteria, wired on acid rock, protest
songs, folks singers socially aware &
Vietnam no longer some way out there,
unimaginable place in the back of stamp
albums under French possessions but a
subject for subterranean homesick blues,
songs of sorrow and lamentation for picket
lines & protests, summers of love drowning
in blood, an alcoholic purple haze, secret
agent's orange, mushroom like clouds, what
did it matter? What was that sound? Draft
riots and FBI files, Big Brother & His
Holding Company, register with your draft
board, pick a number & die, Uncle Sam

a skeleton with Death Watch Beetle eyes,
a paranoids worst fears realized, up against
a wall mother fucker, 'it's all over now, baby
blue', 'it's alright now Ma, I'm only bleeding','
'blowing' in the wind,' blues.

"Some velvet morning when I'm straight—"

Sunday at the Marine Bar
watching the Miller beer sign,
neon tracer rounds highlighting
the clock face, stretching out
the mostly-dark behind the bar,
two longneck bottles of beer to
drink from, one for the left,
one for the right, "Gives new
meaning to the phrase: two fisted
drinker," she is saying, "Buy
me one?" "If I had the money,
I'd buy you two." "It's, okay.
I buy back. I always pay my way."
"Take one of these, I haven't touched
either." And she does. Who is she?
Where did she come from? How long
has she been here? Gauguin re-imagined
in terms of a barroom; more like
Van Gogh in composition, Absinthe
Drinkers, Potato Eaters, Self Portraits
from the ruined end of the palette——
She says, "How about a shot? You do
whiskey, don't you?" Like the movie
"They Shoot Horses Don't They"?
Marathon drinking, trying to outdo
the form in the mirror drinking with
you. one to one, knows no limitations——
"Whiskey, Scotch, whatever, nothing clear,
nothing that burns, nothing that changes

color over ice." "Scotch it is. Two more,
please, the good stuff." Whatever that is.
I thought, how many of these had we done?
I have no clue, sinking further into the deep
black hole of my depression, my darkest
imaginings and she with me, grasping
a hold, digging her nails deep into my
bare skin; the snow and the ice outside
pelting the windows, making the roads
impassable, the sidewalks skating rinks,
outside of wherever I am, staring through
cigarette smoke in the Marine Bar or lost in
her arms somewhere, in her dream or mine,
the unimaginable weight of alcohol
pressing us together, pulling us down, an
unknowable face in a bar mirror staring back.

Season of the Witch

His idea of a fun that Winter was
jumping naked from a second story window,
into a six foot high snow bank outside the dorm
window, screaming at the top of his lungs as
he flew and threatening to do it again until,
"He got it right." A blanket, a few blasts
of cheap bong wine, and another stick of primo
Cambodian Red and he was flying right,
wrapped in some blankets and seeing
the kind of flying monkeys who came for people
who didn't live righteous lives; visions that,
obviously, had nothing to do with him.
Someone suggested taking a spin in his wheels,
the used hearse in the parking lot along with
all the others, "No man, it's cursed. She put
a hex on it." She was the witch he'd been screwing
since he arrived on campus two years ago as
a second semester transfer freshman, with hair
down to his ass and the most dynamic
sound system in a way-beyond-it's-useful-life,
rig. "Man, everyone has a hearse. It's the 60's.
Or a Beetle. But mine has a reel to reel."
A game breaker for a witch who rode shot gun with
the devil, always in black, pentagram amulets and
wild gypsy hair, dead things in her crocheted
shoulder bag along with great weed, mystery powders,
and spell casting shit. "That girl was wild, Man.
beautiful and a heart stopping body once you got
rid of all those clothes. I don't even think she, like

owned, underwear. Only goes with guys who have
a hearse. Says she dug the vibes. And the music.
Man, I loved her but she blew me off. Said I was
dragging her down. Stole all my Donovan tapes.
"Season of the Witch"; that's her life story."
It would have been funny if everyone hadn't seen her
around, climbing in and out of those vehicles,
late at night and the sound of things dying inside
that could never have been misinterpreted as something
else.

Coming Home 1968

No one had to ask,
"Where have you been?"
nights he broke free
from the compound/house,
parents secured, that is locked
in their bedroom, all lines
of communication severed,
illegal weapon set on lock
and load as he readied himself
for a solitary patrol dressed in
full camo and black face paint
using light of a quarter moon
to lead the way down Garfield
Place to the jungle on Ocean
Ave where Charlie was dug in,
sleeping, just four blocks
from home and a half a world,
half a lifetime away.

Late 60's Young America

We were so used to
death, an assassination
was an occasion for
an unexpected holiday,
classes cancelled, books
thrown aside, stereos
turned up as joints rolled,
beer bottles cracked open,
body counts in overseas
jungle as unreal as riots
in the street in nowhere
New York, Utica, where
Nixon's silent majority
ruled & long haired students
on drugs were what was wrong
with America, not the War,
not killing Civil Rights
leaders, not spying on
your fellow citizens, not
shooting candidates for
high office; Death was
a spontaneous party,
taking the blind guys to
the driving range, teeing up
their balls & showing them
where to hit, the arc of a
well struck shot a white
tracer round disappearing
into the clinging mists,

into unreal klieg light haze
over dried brown grass,
over us all, drunk, stoned,
oblivious, young dead men
walking.

"Drugs, Sex and Rock n' Roll"

were the core values of his life,
though it became quite clear
DC was mainly in the game
for the drugs

Was the kind of guy, pumping coins
into the Wurlitzer, would drop
a quarter and looking for his coin
find a gram of pure black Moroccan
hash stuffed behind the record machine

Wouldn't do anything, go anywhere
unless it was all the way, was a moving
target with a hookah for those rare
times he actually stood still

Every weekend with him was an out
of body experience, a dream state
amphetamine fueled experience trying
not to freak because of too much stimulation,
no sleep, musically exploring a dark side
of the moon long before there was an album
that took you there and left you behind,
helpless and alone

As DC would in strange redneck bars, way
out in the sticks, no hope of a ride home
or five miles high and rising in some mother's
of invention state park closed for the season

or in a condemned as unsafe warehouse/fire hazard
twilit zone, the first scent of smoke already in the air

You knew better than to tell him how you survived,
how you escaped, in case you had to do it again

Maybe that's why we were friends; I was the escape
artist he could never be, engaged to death as he was,
eventually rushing head on into her arms doing
a million miles an hour

People ask me what it was like back then
and all I can say is, "I escaped."
I'm still escaping

Visions of Johanna

I don't remember the first time
I saw her

Not exactly
The last few years of the 60's are one long,
stoned, alcoholic blur of darkened bars,
concert venues, frat houses subterranean
homesick blues

"Sunshine of Your Love"
the song of doomed youth I most recall,
her saying, "You look like Donovan.
Before he sold his soul to a record label."

But what I was had more to do, had more
in common with being an exploding ticket
holder on a drunken boat to nowhere
drinking because I was depressed,
the more I drank the more depressed I was,
than actually selling my soul

I was thinking she was some kind
of acid angel who could rescue me from hell
on an endless weekend afternoon of substance
abuse and self pitying gestures that made me
feel as pathetic as I was

Could see her pied beauty face across a dance floor,
barroom, streaked by strobe lights and day glo paints,

coming colors in my mind and I thought
I could reach out and touch her but when I went to
touch, she wasn't there

She wasn't anywhere, was lost in some electric
lady land dream of the 60's, a stolen muse,
a siren song; sometimes I wonder if she was real

Electioneering in the Boondocks 1968

What was Hubert
Humphrey to us
in '68? Some hack
loser, a balding suit,
so way beyond 30,
no one would ever
trust him, just another
war escalator only
nominally less evil
than Nixon, tainted by
Johnsonian blood, but
we'd go see him if he
came to town and he
would, we did go,
gloriously stoned to,
the aptly named War
Memorial, primed for
the opening act doing
medleys of Top 40 Hits:
Hanky Panky, Crimson
and Clover, Hony Mony,
stuff we'd heard before,
live even, having snuck
back stage their last
time in town to hang
out, so way past stoned
and comical, they'd dedicate
a number for the boys
in the back room, now

they were an opening
act for a big show, reality,
politics as usual, riots in
the streets, even in Utica,
cops wearing their America
Love It or Leave It buttons,
badges, busting heads with
billy clubs while those
inside start a chant:
"Dump the Hump!
Dump the Hump!"
the youth vote lost
in a haze of alcohol
and pot.

Trout Fishing in America's

cover: a long-haired hippie
and his woman, suggested
the Aquarian Age, Woodstock,
Free Love, drugs, rock n roll,
all the good things the sixties
had to offer we were leaving
behind in the new dark ages
of Nixon, Altamont, Charlie
Manson, wars of containment
by attrition, police state riot
gears, Maxwell's silver hammer
of death, all the baggage DC
carried within him as a silent
soon-to-be-killer, a suicidal
disease no one recognized
until it was way too late.
He picked up my Brautigan, sd.,
"These people look really
blissed out. Happy and free."
Lifted the book along with
the poetry text he was borrowing
for a class he'd attend on
different drugs, determined by
phases of the moon, all his
favorite rock stars dead or dying,
along the twisted mined super-
highway in his head that divided
him in two like some kind of
blacktopped Mekong swollen by

monsoon and atrocity kills he felt
obligated to explore, fishing with
hand grenades, hot shrapnel in his
brain, a lure for later, when life
got seriously fucked driving blind
and crazy, way beyond alcohol
and drugs. When all the shit hit
I wondered how far into the trout
stream he had gone and which dead
rock star was going with him
to that no exit place of no U-turns,
no reverse, no get out of jail free

This is "The End" 1968

Long before "The End" was made into something like an icon;
Long before Apocalypse Now! used the words, the voice, the
images to frame a movie that took "Heart of Darkness" one step
further into the jungle;

Long before the politics of South East Asia were revealed as a
mixture of nightmare and the grotesque, were a long drawn out,
drugged out, alcoholic trip;

Long before the lead singer of the group that made 'The End'
became the Lizard King and everything he wrote, said, sang,
performed became a kind of prophetic wisdom for a doomed
generation, hooked up to a rage machine, a chain gang of
self indulgence, altered conceptions, back alley incantations,
dream worlds dissolving into mind altering memories lying just
beyond the doors of perception;

Long before "Light My Fire" scaled the charts to the top and the
album following close behind,

We were midnight warriors of lost causes and substance abuse,
following the blood stained hallways of the dormitory and of the
mind to remove the faces from the ancient gallery and DC,
the pusher man, was the master demon handing out smoke of many
dreams laced with hallucinatory angel's dust not bothering to recite
required warning labels that said:

Borderline personalities should not mess with mind altering drugs;
these same minds skidding over the edge with Eldridge Cleaver's

Soul on Ice to some strange black lit place where Jimbo was God,
his psychedelic poster dead center in the revolving ceiling,
his eyes controlling all the respiratory muscles of those who have
entered here, those who are spinning out of control, lost in some
twisted dreams of mad mandala, transcendent spaces within
dissolving rainbows;

And the black light was everything then, divine light flickering within
Jimbo's Godhead eyes, the passageway to another world, another
existence, time and place revealed as a ruined Temple of a Thousand
Columns that lay just beyond the killing fields of play and of war, all
the sacrificial victims of the mind being dropped into the sacred
sinkholes, weighted down by baubles, by jewels and scarce items
for trade in another world of vanished gods and goddesses, those
sacrificed not so much murdered as offered an involuntary
conveyance to another world presumed better than this one;

Where chronology is marked on the four-sided altars, pyramids
built one atop the other, re-enforced from within, seasons precisely
marked on carved without metal tools, stone faces of futility, fertility
symbols, writhing snakes illuminated by a directness of sun, light
that amplifies, signifies, suggests the coming of the Lizard King
dressed in form fitting leather pants, matching black vest, silk shirt
open to the waist to reveal the scars of rank, the painted emblems
of his kind as he assumes the mask of his trade, summoning fireballs
from the sky, the rolling fireballs that lay waste to the jungle,
bringing the black light that makes day into night, his caustic,
his causative tongue and ravaged voice amplified
to a point that inspires terror in this afflicted place we are walking
through, ceremonial knives unsheathed, this place once a home,
now, 'The End.'

Walking Home Winter 1970

fog rising
from semi-frozen

fields: pale white
on slush grey;

feet leaving
post holes behind

stuck half way
to nowhere

after last call;
blinking lights

in the otherwise
dark, a disused

building, former
asylum, home to

no one and no thing,
disabled wheelchairs

and hospital beds
locked inside,

bars still on
the windows

Number 9 Dream, Just Before Finals, Winter 1969

After all the cafes have been
closed, the beatniks busted,
hipsters, gone cats, have all switched
from smoke to hooch, three piece
suits, suburban commutes and thirty
year mortgage nightmares,
only the black walls and hollow
shells of the fifties left behind.
Happening bistros are now dive
bars with names like Horny Toad,
Happy Hobbit, Emergency Room,
graffito encouraged in black light
back rooms, glow in the dark phrases:
"Bombing for Peace is like fucking
for chastity", "War is not good for
children and other living things",
"Sterilize LBJ-No more ugly children".
Slogans fading in real light around
last call, overseas war images on
black and white TV at end of well-
carved, cigarette burned bar.
Doors "Crystal Ship" segues into
Jim Hendrix, "All Along the
Watchtower", long haired, dead end
crew's, final shooters for the road
washed down with warm, flat beer.
Outside, snow falling, a foot on
the ground and more to come,
nowhere to come from here but
home, nowhere to go but down.

Our Big Night at the Movies, Utica, 1969

Thursday night, one showing only
double features: Russ Meyer,
quadruple Double D babes,
Flesh Gordon takeoffs, soft porn
with a sense of humor, underbelly
of Hollywood stars and starlets:
Cynthia Myers, Long Dong Silver,
Donna Does It, John Hardwood,
Betty Boobs. Posted: No Alcohol Allowed
sleazoid theater, beverages snuck in
by the six pack in oversized,
multi-pocket, Army surplus jackets.
Weed smoking in Men's Room timed
piss breaks, "a little weed will do ya",
shifts. Ushers paid not to really care
or notice, dirty old men and long haired
college students, as long as they don't
burn the place down. Extra charge
for Special Foreign Import Features"
"Carmen Baby", "My Sister, My Love",
Fanny's Hill". All almost as boring
as Carmen's whore friend chewing gum
and talking on the phone as she got laid.
Still, Carmen and extra long necked Chianti
bottle, was the best thing on stage anyone
had seen since The Inferno burned down.
Ugly hooker working parking lot after flicks,
group rates available, "I've got the real
stuff you boys are looking for."

"Hold that thought, Sweetheart,"
exit lines as cars sped off, mid-term
exams, overdue papers, Vietnam War,
could wait for another day, another
week of cheap beer and Mary Jane,
Oh, Sweet, Merciful Mary Jane.

Romancing the 60's: with lines from Charles Bukowski

The weekends that began earlier each week
and ended later;
the new drugs and the old, turning on,
dropping out, going more than a
little crazy;
the war that never seemed to end and our
friends who went to fight and
never came back;
their letters in a shoebox with the rolling
papers and the love beads, black arm
bands with peace signs, draft notices
to appear;
risk taking on the highways, everyone behind
the wheel A Rebel Without a Cause,
a Wild One with no sense of direction,
a MASH unit in a snow bank, dead
of winter, blood rock and frostbite;
shooting pool in some redneck bar on the edge
of Deliverance not afraid to die;
stoned crazy to acid rock, 8 miles high and falling
fast, writing it all down and forgetting
how to read;
The White Album and the Number 9;
Our Lady of Gone Tomorrows, an ex-barefoot nun
with a tambourine and a jug of California
white, collecting quarters to buy a map back
home, to find the key to the Lost Silver Mines
of nowhere;

Helter Skelter and the zombie chicks from Hell;
A bad trip, a bummer, run, run the Homecoming
    Queen's got a gun;
Pistol Pete and the tail gunner geek killing machine
    living next door, out of uniform but not out
      of the jungle and he doesn't know what to do;
"it was a romantic grand game then, full of the fury
    of discovery" Bukowski would say.

"I read the books about the lives of the boys"

The Crack Up....

Bathtub Gin, champagne cocktails
for breakfast in the afternoon, soldier boy
prophets on the Boardwalk, on Park Place,
Dreaming of Daisy, stumbling drunk,
pyromanic, kleptomanic, crazy as sewer rats
in drag; flapper girls and the Charleston,
Uptown and Down, the far off red light
on the Sound.

Death in the Afternoon.
The Black Sun and the smell of cordite
in the morning, Cole Porter riffs, champagne
and a double suicide pact, masked balls
and an open vein marriage of heaven and
hell, blood baths and

Death in the Afternoon
This Side of Paradise
The Beautiful and the Damned
An American Tragedy
Being Geniuses Together
A Moveable Feast
Three Soldiers
and The Bridge

An American in Paris

Side Cars and Cuba Libre
The Love Songs of Alice B. Toklas and
Gertrude Stein
Death in the Afternoon
Trench Warfare and ambulance driving
50 Sunshine Superman
The Enormous Room and
A Farewell to Arms

The Sun Also Rises
in no man's land and well beyond
Death in the Afternoon
Que es mas macho?

The man with the double barreled shotgun
in his mouth
or the one with the bullet in his head?

Summer of Love

Lightning over the water,
over the docks where inboards
are moored in their slips,
sailboats battened down for
the inevitable storm and inside
the vine covered house, Gracie
and The Airplane are singing,
"When the truth is found, to be lies,
and all the love within you dies——"
pot smoke as thick as candle wax
on the wicker based Chianti bottles,
so strange to be 18 going on 19,
strange as the surrealistic pillow
sounds, the images of Nam jungle
of never ending war, all hell broken
loose on sound-turned-off tube in
the darkness, naked to the waist,
blowing excellent demon weed and
washing it away with flat Filipino
beer, San Miguel and M., one fucked up
chick on a mission to burn baby burn
like a city, like Newark in flames,
Vanilla Fudge dropping down onto
the turn table, "You keep me hanging on—"
in half time, a warped acid freaked
chorus of long haired angels singing
and playing for the dead and the soon-
to-be dead, M. exhaling a lung full
of weed in my face, leaning closer as

if to kiss; race riots in one eye, jungle
war scenes in the other, rolling thunder
all around.

"in the story he tells, the cold is the truth"

Erica Wagner

He said, "You've never lived until you've been dead."
I agreed
After all it was his bottle we were drinking out of
I agreed
Even though I had no idea what he was talking about

"Ever smoke a roll your own?" He asked
"No, man. Can't we go somewhere else to do this? I'm freezing
my ass off."
"We could. Smoke this and it won't matter."
So we did and he was right

It didn't matter that it was who-knew-what-time after midnight,
ten below out there among the yews and the family
crypts and the monuments to war heroes and patriots
so long forgotten the mold had claimed their family names

It didn't matter that the wind was blowing so hard it
would make a banshee hoarse when she screamed
and washing away the taste required more sweet wine
that either of us cared to think about

"You ever know anyone who died?" He asked
"Sure, man. Who hasn't?"
"I mean like our age?"
"Shit, yeah. There's a war on, haven't you heard?"
It was 1968

Guys our age were dying all the time

"Why do you think we're here?" He said."Smoking this shit
if not to forget about that damned war. And a whole lot of
everything else too."

"Well, it's working big time. I can barely move."
"You'd better be able to. You're way too heavy to carry and I
don't just mean how much your body weighs."
"Very funny."
"I'm serious, I'd leave you here if I had to. Who knows when
they'd miss you. Or when they'd find you. I'm sure as hell
not coming back here. Nor for you or anyone else. Not alive anyway."
I laughed, thinking he was kidding
And he laughed as well, knowing he was not

A few years later he offed himself in a spectacular way.
Took a few with him too. Who knew what he was thinking
when he checked out or if he was thinking at all

Looking back, I think it was like 50/50 whether he brought
me out to that graveyard
to die with him or just to get stoned out of our minds
It didn't seem to make much difference to him
Maybe he just thought, it just wasn't the day to die

Desolation Angels

for DC

Remember how it was back in
the swinging 60's? forty eight hours
of drinking that began on Friday
afternoon and didn't end until
the last keg ran dry, wherever we
were, whenever it was? Sleep
a foreign concept like Vietnam,
we had to keep our grades up in
order to survive, had to keep going
even when the double yellow lines
on the frozen highways of upstate
New York began to converge or
veer off into the dark unknown
beyond all the lost highways we
wandered weekends that might
never end, you and me and Doc
and anyone who could still stand,
who could still light the high grade
weed we blew just to take that bloated
drunk edge off and if we showed signs
of wavering, going down for the count,
about to crash, DC would be handing
out industrial strength speed, calling
us his favorite desolation angels,
dharma bums on a bad trip through
the living karmic hell he was creating
for us to get lost in, calling our last-
men-standing gonzo staying power,

strength of the gods, anything but
what it was, a public execution,
he would be around to clean up after,
collecting trinkets from the bodies
of the dead to be preserved in a private
museum, sarcophagi for sunset supermen
he doled out to his latest hippie chick
converts calling them relics of a dying
age; the sixties man, remember how it
was? what a blast man, we were lucky
to survive.

"like the songs you used to hear on late-night radio"

Late night FM radio in the 60's,
no cool jazz or silly little love songs,
no top 40's hits, bubblegum music
or Montovani but real cuts from deep
inside the political scene, unrest and
protest, music from the mud at Woodstock,
from the killing fields of Kent State,
pagan princes, stoned goddesses,
acid rockers tripping through city
streets eight miles high and falling
fast the Altamont horror like a chainmail
monkey on their backs. Killer lyrics
and dead rock stars, doom sayers of
a police state, military-industrial complex
out of control, righteous music of long
haired hippie heads blissed out way past
midnight on the promise-of-sex-blessed voice
of Alison the Nightbird, WNEW on your dial,
free form radio: whole sides of Sergeant Pepper,
Moody Blues, Clapton and Cream, Bonnie
and Delany, Yardbirds and Crosby Steals
the Cash and Runs, maybe some Monk
and Miles mixed in, music to burn draft cards
and flags to, music for making bombs,
music to die for.

Down and Out in Clinton, N.Y. with Chicago and a Quote from Dylan's 'Sad Eyed Lady of the Lowlands'

It was the winter of
living in the wake
of Steinbeck novel
titles, The Winter of
Our Discontent, Grapes
of Wrath, East of Eden——,
cast out of paradise to
roam the frozen steppes
of upstate New York
enclosed by a second
ice age that lasted longer
than Richard Three's dis-
content, stumbling drunk
and disorderly, three times
stoned, and finding yourself
in dim lighted hockey arena,
rank with sweat of enforcer
ringers on skates and body
armor like Rollerball warriors
disguised as athletes, brawling
their way to championships
with conventional weapons
of the trade, hard drinking
afterwards, one step ahead
of the local police, bail bonds-
men and landlords. A filmy
haze lifting off a glaze of,

covered over for an event, ice,
meeting a density of cigarette
smoke and somewhere within
auxiliary light, the hottest rock
band on the charts running
through their riffs, four part
harmonies, strings: lead guitars,
rhythm, bass, horns, percussion,
vocals an overwhelming speed

rush and extra adrenaline high
that can only be tempered after-
ward with depth charging
boilermakers, total oblivion,
riding a roller coaster with
both hands strapped to a metal
rod, feeling out cold pockets
of hell, out of control in a
void where dreams should go
filling up with subzero wind
chill, snow and ice; the emptiness
that follows growing with each
numbing swallow, each gasp
of air, and all 'these sheet metal
memories of Cannery Row."

Walking Home in Winter, Utica, N.Y. 1969

Past houses down dark streets,
across drift rifted fields
ice rimmed, hard crusted,
hip high in places; down sleet
slickened streets, beneath
bare looming trees, between
ruined tenement rows, dead
sick on piles of frozen crap,
garbage heaps dragged from
black plastic, breath thick as
the iced houses, burned out,
yellow taped over collapsed
facades, drooping porches,
glass windows, doors, punched
out, axed into oblivion, shattered
wooden frames hanging from
twisted, rusted nails; down dark
streets, shot out light bulbs, long
twisted veins electrical cording
attached to nothing; by the long
bodies of hearses jammed into
traffic circles, up against high curbs,
neon strip club signs signaling
a distant life somewhere beyond
the red cross painted doors, the white
flagged, plague houses.

Beneath the Wheel 1970

Life in that year was a traveling
circus for him, an experience
somewhere between a religious
conversion and a mystical vision
of demons and devils competing
for first crack at a mind already raging
out of control with a draft notice
in one hand and an invitation to
appear at Whitehall Street in NYC
for a physical that could be the major
determining factor as to whether
the next few years would become an
expense paid jungle vacation in
South East Asia or studying another
corpus, the dead white men also known
as the major English authors; began
living in a gulf somewhere between
being a kind of blind leading the blind
student teacher of disaffected youth,
and the living dead, becoming a
different kind of walking casualty/
work in progress as an unemployed,
unemployable long hair/ walking stress
machine on the edge of a precipice
of an inherited schizophrenic malaise
exacerbated by depression especially
now that a child had been born and another
was on the way; he wasn't quite broken on
the wheel of life but was riding on the rim of
the blown spare, half way to hell and asking
directions for how to get all the way there.

"The last drink is best,"

he said as we drove North
in the night, windows wide open,
dead of winter long white outside,
car heater on full blast, a fifth of
Calvert's Rye for two, and a twelve
pack of Fort Schuyler beer in cans,
maybe the last of their kind, we drank,
completely stoned on angel dust weed,
the wind some kind of gale force,
whipping our shoulder length hair
in our faces, so ossified, neither of us
could have blinked if we wanted to.
Driving on, barely retaining the sense of sight,
barely seeing the faint lights in
by-the-side-of-the-road houses,
businesses, speeding by like broken
white lines on the wavering highway,
"Where we headed? I asked, yelling
to make myself heard above the rush of wind,
feeling the needles of ice and frozen snow
stinging our faces as we moved further North.
"Doesn't matter." he said. "Pass me some
of that piss water, I need something wet
on my tongue. It feels frozen like my brain."
"Yeah, man, I feel it too.
Hey, man, speedometer looks broken, it's off
the board."
"Yeah, it does that. Don't worry. Who needs
to know that shit anyway?"

There was nothing I could think of to say
so I handed him another beer.
I didn't know where we were going but
I knew it wouldn't be long before we got there.

for DC RIP

1970

They act as if you were
born old, some kind of
Ancient of Days with a
shot glass, say, "Do you
remember 1970?"
And you zone out into
a hard rain is gonna fall
moment, Spring semester
senior year, stoned crazy
since some forgotten time
in the Fall of 1969,
vaguely recalling listening
to Sun Ra record in dark
of Sunset Blvd. duplex
amenable to any suggestion,
even ones that don't make
sense, maybe especially
those, "Let's go to the
reservoir and listen to
the water going over
the dam—"in torrential
rain, sliding down steep
embankment, the mud and
the grass underfoot, Hinkley
runoff, a virtual Niagara
of sound and power, all
the clinging mud some kind
of strange prelude to, not so
far away prospect of Basic

of being shipped overseas
into the jungle, part of a
new Credence tune, "Better
run through the jungle——
Don't look back—"into
the rain, the swirling torrents
debating whether to jump
now and be done with it or
join the living dead, dog
soldiers on this mission
that serves no purpose,
the interior car light a beacon
beckoning in the distance
"A bad moon risin'———
Who'll stop the rain——
Proud Mary keeps on burning
rolling on the river——"
hit parade of Credence tunes
intimations of mortality,
an impetus to make the climb,
the long journey home.
Inside the car, bone cold,
shivering, lighting another
stick for the road pounded
flat as all the double lines
we crossed over, living all
the worst kind of bad dreams
a man could want——"
"1970," I said, "Yeah, I
remember 1970, A great year
for Sports, Drugs and Rock
and Roll."